A WONDERFUL GIFT

SOLVE THE REBUS AND SEE THE WONDERFUL GIFT THAT GOD WANTS TO GIVE YOU.

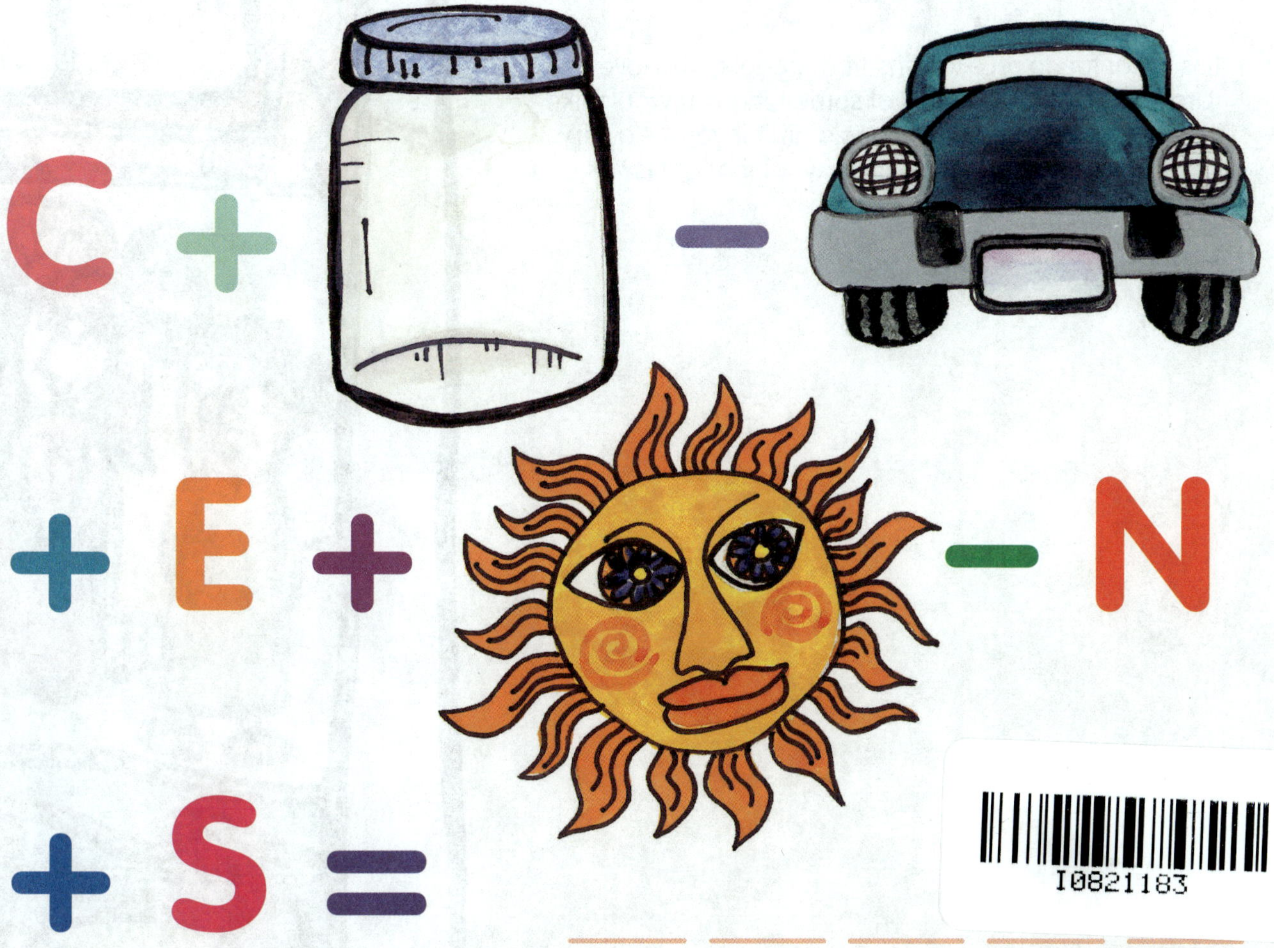

C + [jar] – [car]

+ E + [sun] – N

+ S = ___ ___ ___ ___ ___

by *Francine M. O'Connor*

Lesson 2

A GIFT IS SOMETHING SPECIAL

It is great fun to receive gifts from people who love you. Draw a picture in this box of something you would like to receive as a gift. Jesus has a gift for you — a very special gift. Do you know what that gift is?

A Gif

I AM

JESUS SHOWS HIS LOVE!

Jesus came to teach about God's love.
He told his apostles to let the little children come to him.
He said that a child's love is a special kind of love and all God's people should love as children do.

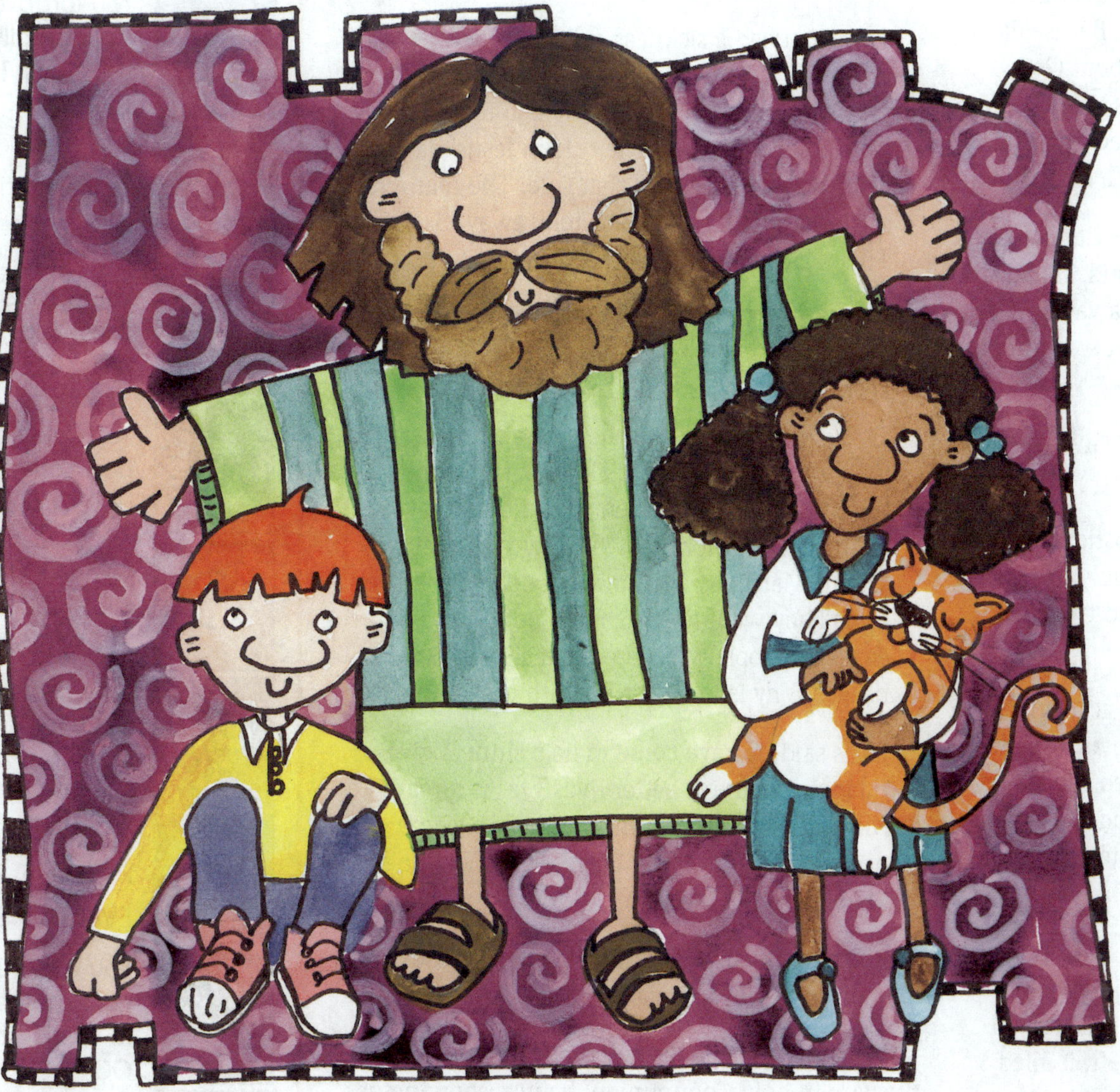

by Francine M. O'Connor

Stories of Jesus

The best stories are stories about Jesus and his love. These are three especially good ones.

JESUS FEEDS THE PEOPLE

Luke 9:10-17

One day, Jesus was speaking to thousands of people in a far-away place called Bethsaida. He spoke about God the Father's love. The people stayed and listened for a long time.

The apostles came to Jesus and said, "Send the people away now so they can get something to eat."

Jesus said, "Give them food to eat."

But the apostles replied, "We have only five loaves of bread and two fish."

Then Jesus said, "Have the people sit down." The apostles did as Jesus said. Jesus blessed the loaves and fish, and the apostles gave them to the people.

The people ate and ate and ate until they were all full. When the apostles picked up what was left, it filled 12 baskets! This was a miracle of love.

JESUS HELPS THE SICK

Matthew 8:1-4

One day, a sick man came to Jesus. He wanted Jesus to cure him. Jesus said, "I will do it. Be cured." He touched the man and right away, the man was all better.

This man had a sickness called leprosy. People would not go near a leper because they thought they'd get sick too. The lepers had to stay away from town. That was the rule in Jesus' day. Jesus didn't care about that rule. The man was sick and hurting and Jesus took away his pain. This was another miracle of love.

JESUS FORGIVES SINNERS

Matthew 9:9-13

This is the story of Matthew, a tax collector who was not well liked. He took tax money from the poor even when they did not have enough money for food. "Follow me," Jesus said to Matthew. Matthew got up and followed him. They went to Matthew's house to eat. The people whispered and shook their heads."Why is Jesus eating with that sinner?"

Jesus said, "I have come to help sinners give up their sins and live better lives." Jesus forgave Matthew and loved him. Matthew became one of Jesus' apostles. He followed Jesus for the rest of his life.

Jesus' forgiveness is a miracle of love. Jesus showed his love in many ways.

When he gave us his own body and blood to share in holy Communion, he was showing us his love. While you are preparing to receive your first holy Communion, remember how much Jesus loves you.

A JESUS KIND OF LOVE

Jesus showed his love for people by feeding the hungry, healing the sick, and forgiving sinners. Here is a game to help you learn how to love as Jesus loved. You will need two buttons and a coin. Flip the coin to see how many spaces you will move. Heads, move two spaces; tails, move one. The spaces will tell you how to love with a Jesus kind of love.

You forgave a friend who accidentally broke one of your toys. TAKE ANOTHER TURN.

SKIP TO THE NEXT BUG.

You gave some of your allowance to help feed the poor. GO AHEAD 3 SPACES.

You said something to hurt someone's feelings. LOSE A TURN.

GO TO THE HIGH-FIVE CORNER AND GIVE EVERYONE A HIGH FIVE.

Your sister said she was sorry for hurting you, but you would not listen to her. GO BACK TO START.

GO TO THE HUG CORNER AND GIVE EVERYONE A HUG.

You were grumpy when your mother asked you to clean up your room. GO BACK 1 SPACE.

GO TO THE SMILE CORNER AND SMILE.

"This Is My Body"

Jesus loves you so much he wants to share his life with you.
Before he died, Jesus found a very special way to live in your heart forever.
Do you know what that way was?
Unscramble these letters to discover a way to have
Jesus in your heart all the time.

OHYL

____

OMCMUINNO

____

by Francine M. O'Connor

Lesson 3

A LOVE-MEAL WITH JESUS

When Jenny's friend Tom was moving, his mother gave a farewell party for Tom and his friends. Jenny didn't want to go. "I don't want Tom to leave," she said.

Her mother said, "Tom is your best friend. Remember the good times you had? Your friendship will last as long as your memories last."

Then Jenny's mother told her about Jesus' farewell party. It was the night before he died. He invited his friends to a meal. Like Jenny, they were very sad. It was to be their last supper together.

Jesus spoke many words of love. He asked the Father to take care of all his friends in the world. He promised that he would return. He would never leave them alone.

Jesus gave his friends a sign. He took bread and blessed it, saying,

"This is my body."

He passed the bread around for all to share. Later, he took wine and said,

"This is my blood."

He passed the cup around and said,

"Do this in memory of me."

The next day Jesus died on the cross. On the wonderful Sunday we call Easter, Jesus returned to his friends — just as he had promised. He stayed for a little while, then went to his Father in heaven. Jesus' friends always remembered that wonderful Last Supper meal. Instead of a sad farewell party, it was really a celebration! Death could not take Jesus away. He was there in the bread and wine. They never forgot his words: "This is my body...This is my blood."

Here comes the very best part! Jesus Christ is with you today in holy Communion. What a super gift Jesus gives. The gift of *himself* forever.

A TIME TO REMEMBER AND CELEBRATE

Family celebrations are fun. There is a special time for all of God's family to come together and celebrate the gift that Jesus gave to us before he died, the gift of himself. Solve the rebus to find out the name of our celebration.

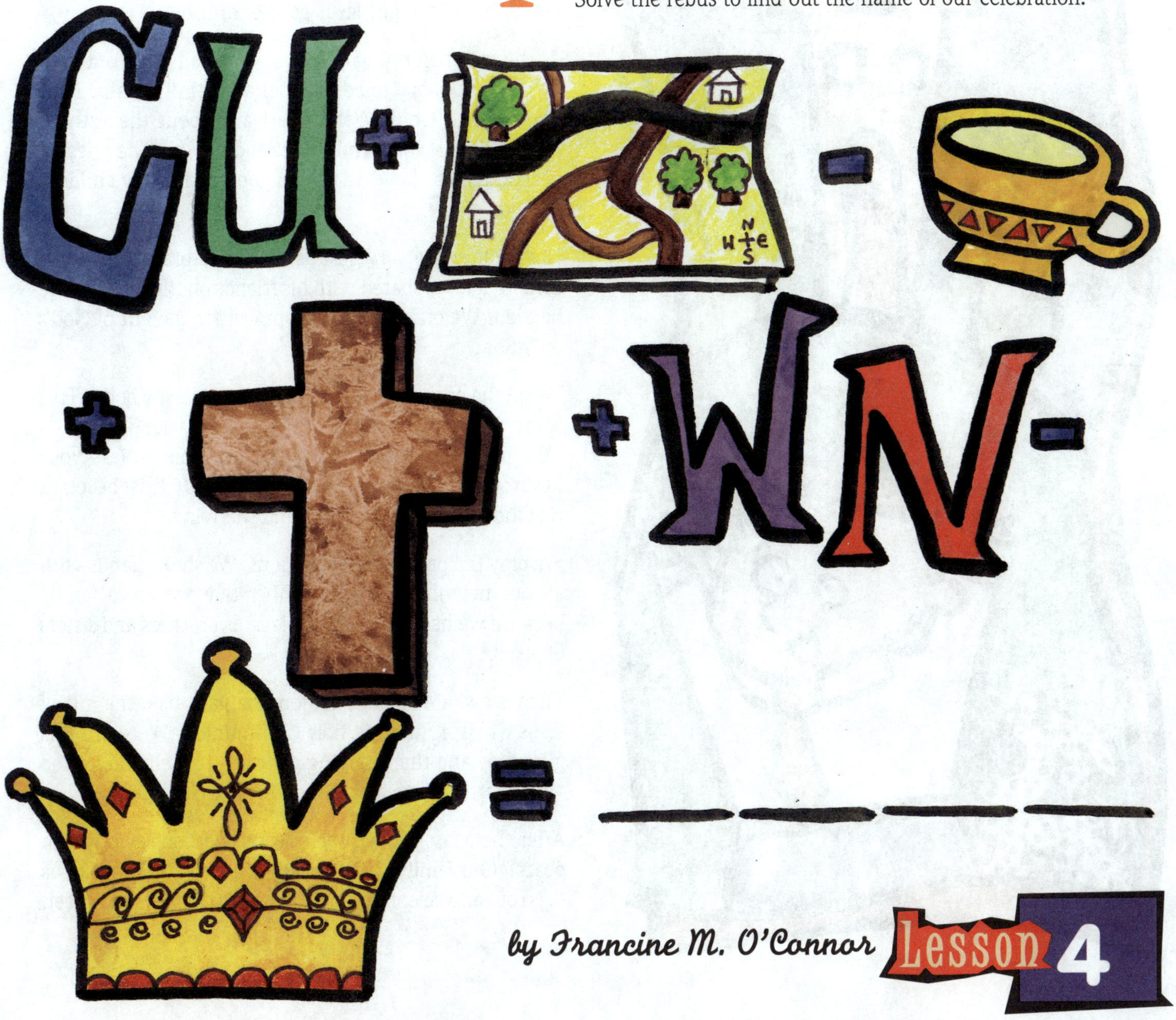

CU + [map] - [cup] + [cross] + WN - [crown] = _ _ _ _ _ _ _ _ _ _

by Francine M. O'Connor

Lesson 4

A Family Celebration

On a special, happy day, how does your family celebrate? Do you have a party? Do you share a special meal? Do you pray together? Do you talk and remember good times? Do you sing and hug and laugh? Do you sometimes exchange gifts? Family celebrations are fun! They are filled with family love.

Do you know how the family of God celebrates together? They come together in Mass to sing and talk and remember God and the gift Jesus gave of himself.

At the very beginning of Mass, we usually sing out with joy. We are happy to be together as a family again. Then we listen to God's Word. We learn about the Father's love. We hear wonderful stories about Jesus. The priest or deacon tells us how we can be good and happy children of God.

Now comes the very best part. We celebrate the special meal that Jesus shared with his friends on the night before he died. We pray a thank-you prayer for the gift of God's only Son.

When the priest says Jesus' words: "This is my body...This is my blood," we remember the happy Easter surprise—"We proclaim your Death, O Lord, and profess your Resurrection until you come again." Jesus Christ becomes real food for us in the bread and the wine.

We pray the prayer Jesus taught us. We shake hands with all our neighbors. We remember that we are a family because we have all been baptized as brothers and sisters of Jesus.

Then we share the special food he gave us—the gift of Jesus Christ himself in holy Communion. We share this gift in joy and thanksgiving, for the gift itself and for the "togetherness" we feel as members of God's family.

After the Mass is over, the priest or deacon says, "Go in peace." Our family celebration does not end. It's time for us to go out and celebrate God's love with everyone we meet.

First COMMUNION
PREPARING CHILDREN FOR THE SACRAMENT OF THE EUCHARIST

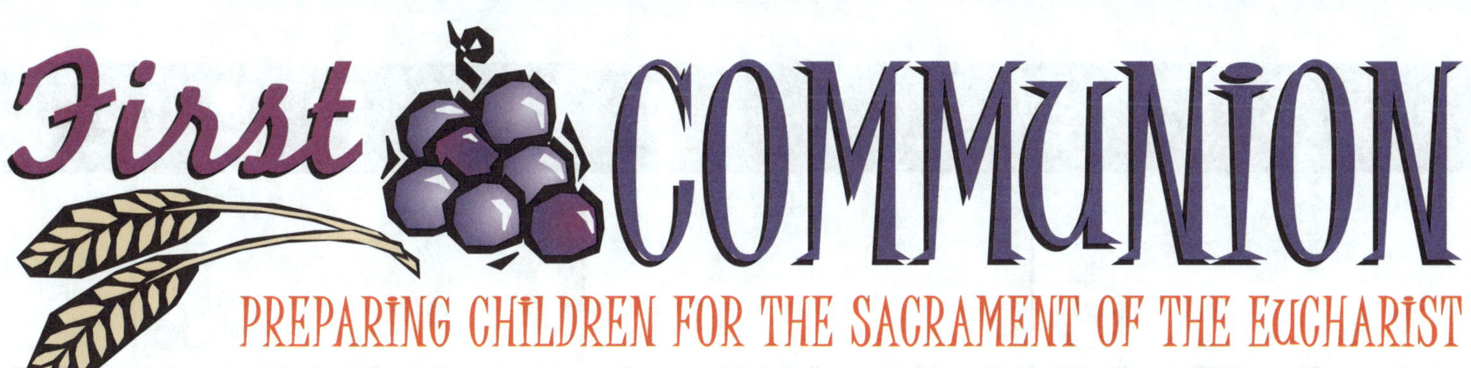

A LITTLE HOUSE IN BETHANY

based on Luke 10:38-42

There's a little house in Bethany,
with smooth, white stones along the walk
and a cozy fireplace inside
where good friends gather around to talk.

This is the home of Jesus' friends,
Mary and Martha and Lazarus.
One day when Jesus came to call,
Martha jumped up and began to fuss.

She took out the kettle and set it to boil
and prepared all of Jesus' favorite treats:
wheat bread and honey, fish from the sea,
and spice cakes with tea, hot and sweet.

While Martha worked to prepare this feast,
Mary sat beside Jesus, so quietly,
listening to all that he had to say
about God and heaven and eternity.

"Lord," complained Martha, "can't you see
that Mary has left all the work to me?
Tell her to get up and do her share
of the good things I am doing for you."

"Martha, Martha, you fidget and fuss
about all the work you say you must do.
Be quiet like Mary and hear my words,
for there's so much I want to say to you."

Like Martha, you have so much you must do,
such as helping others and learning to share,
but the very first thing Jesus asks of you
is to be quiet and sit with him in prayer.

Listen to his words when you go to church,
he wants to tell you that he cares for you.
Then go out and share and love and serve,
with Jesus to bless all the good that you do.

by Francine M. O'Connor

Lesson 5

Jesus Calls You to Come

The story about Martha and Mary shows how each of them loved Jesus very much.

They each chose a different way to show Jesus their love. Martha wanted everything to be just right for him. She went straight to the kitchen and started cooking a special meal.

But Mary never left his side. She sat down at his feet. She listened to his stories. She gazed at him with love.

Martha was loving Jesus in a busy way. Mary wanted nothing more than to be close to her Lord.

Jesus said that Mary had chosen the best way! She *listened* to his words. She *showed* him her love. She *remained* by his side. Later she would serve him by following his Word.

Soon you will receive Jesus Christ on your first Communion day. He will come and live in your heart. How will you get ready?

Do as Mary did! First, listen to Jesus' words...then show him all your love by following his commands.

Jesus said, "Love God with all your heart and mind." Love God in your prayers each day. Love God by going to Mass often. Love God by listening to God's Word. Love God by saying you're sorry when you have sinned.

Jesus said, "Love one another as I have loved you." Love Jesus by loving others. Love Jesus by sharing your things. Love Jesus by helping at home. Love Jesus by forgiving others.

Get ready for Jesus to visit. Do as Mary did. First listen to his words and then follow his commands.

First COMMUNION

PREPARING CHILDREN FOR THE SACRAMENT OF THE EUCHARIST

Company for Dinner

Susan's family is having company for dinner. Susan is wearing her best dress. Before dinner, the family prays together to thank God for the good food and for the good company. During dinner, Mother is proud of Susan's good manners. Company for dinner is very special.

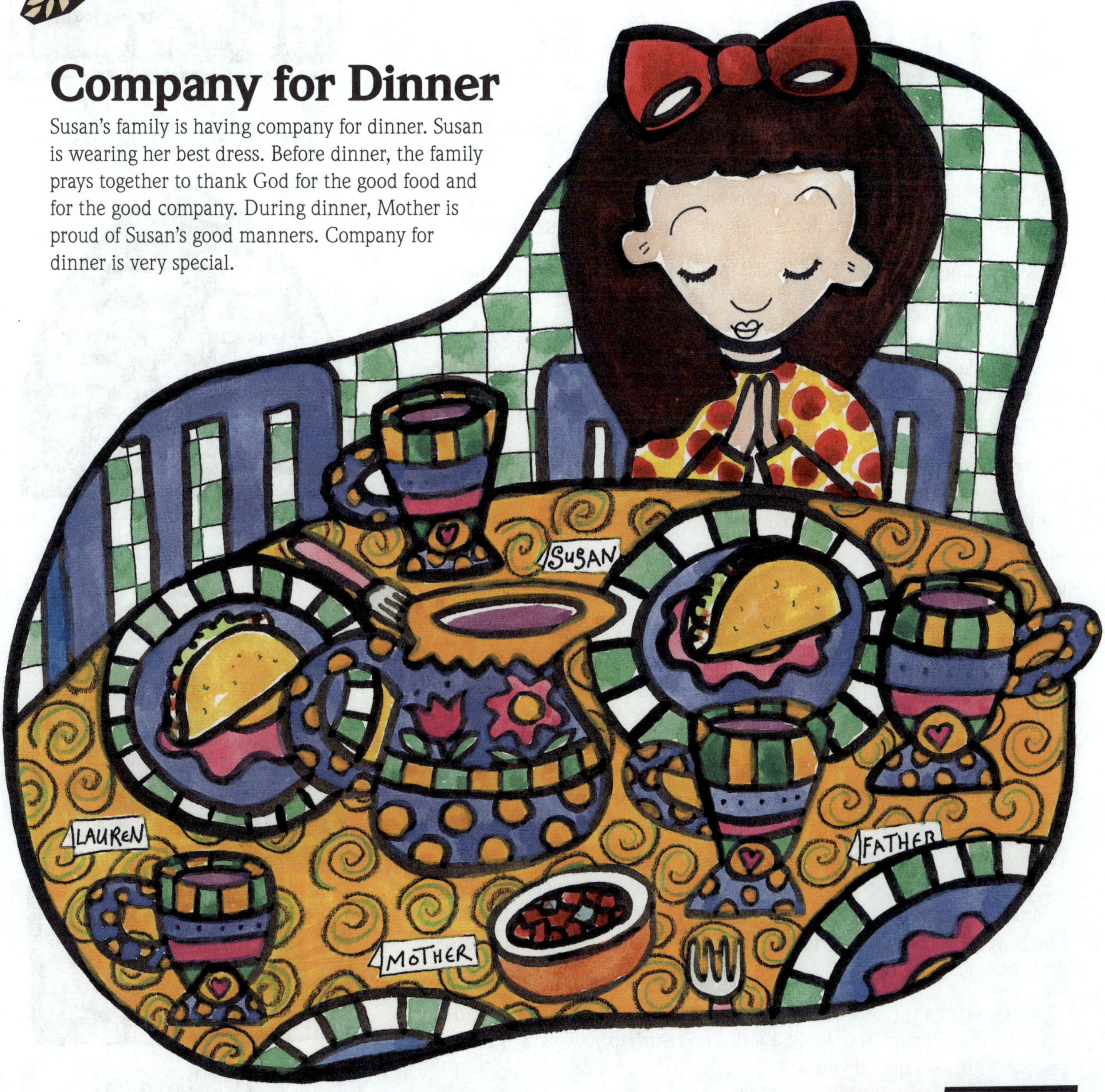

Editor: Lauren K. Borstell • Art and design: Christine Kraus

by Francine M. O'Connor

The Mass...
A Meal With Jesus

Do you remember the story about the Last Supper that Jesus shared with his friends?

Remember when Jesus said, "This is my body...This is my blood..."? After Jesus and his friends ate and drank, he said, "Do this in memory of me."

You are getting ready now for a special meal with Jesus. It is a meal that remembers that Last Supper. Jesus Christ himself will be your food.

To receive Jesus, you have learned to be the very best you can be. You have listened to Jesus' Word. You have followed his commands. You have prayed and told God you are sorry for your sins. God's grace lives in you. Now you are ready for your *first holy Communion!*

To honor Jesus' wonderful gift, you go without eating or drinking for one hour before Communion. (You may take medicine or water within that hour though.) You enter the church with your family and friends. The Mass begins and Jesus comes to you in special ways.

Jesus comes to you in his Word. You listen as the lector reads the stories from the Bible. You listen to the homilist as he talks to you about God.

Jesus comes to you in his people. You offer yourself to Jesus as the gifts are brought to the altar. At the sign of peace, you shake hands with the people sitting near you to show your love for your brothers and sisters in your Church family.

Now it is time to receive Jesus Christ's body and blood for your very first time. What a special moment for you!

You bow your head and pray. When it is your turn, look at the consecrated host and hear the words: "The Body of Christ." Answer, "Amen." "Amen" means, "Yes! I believe this is truly Jesus Christ." You receive the consecrated host in your hand or on your tongue. You chew, swallow, and pray, "Thank you, Jesus, for your love."

If you are offered the consecrated wine, you answer "Amen" to the words, "The Blood of Christ." You swallow a sip and return to your pew to talk to Jesus in your own special words.

Because he loves you so, Jesus gave up his life. Because he loves you so, Jesus lives again within you. What a wonderful gift! Jesus himself is alive in your heart!

"This is my body..."

"This is my blood..."

"Do this in memory of me."

First COMMUNION

PREPARING CHILDREN FOR THE SACRAMENT OF THE EUCHARIST

by Francine M. O'Connor

Lesson 7

Your Church Family

When you were baptized, something wonderful happened! Your parents and your godparents promised to help you grow as a very special child of God. By your baptism, you joined your *Church family.*

With God as your Father, and Jesus as your Brother, all God's people became your family. And they welcomed you as their newest member. Now you have two families — your *home family* and your *Church family.*

Think about ways your home family celebrates special times together. You share a special dinner to celebrate Thanksgiving. You give gifts to each other for birthdays and for Christmas. Maybe you sing and laugh together just because you are happy. And, of course, you worship together to thank God for each other. Special times and celebrations make memories that last forever.

Your Church family wants to share your special times with you, too. That's why, when you make your first holy Communion, your Church family will be there. They will join with you in listening to God's Word. They will be happy with you and sing God's praises with you. And when you receive Communion, they will share the same body and blood. Jesus Christ will live in their hearts just as he will be living in yours.

Saint Paul told God's people, "By sharing in the same loaf of bread [Jesus], we become *one body*, even though there are many of us" (1 Cor 10:17). That one body, of which every member of your Church family is a part, becomes more and more like Jesus every time you receive him in holy Communion. What any one of you does affects that one body. When your whole Church family receives Jesus Christ in Communion with you, you become like one in Jesus. Jesus lives and loves in each of you.

Just think about that! Jesus lives and loves in all those people at once! Jesus makes the world more loving through you and all your family.

FOODS THAT MAKE YOU STRONG

You need all of these foods to help your body grow strong and healthy. If you don't get enough of them, you will soon become very weak. You might even get sick. Unscramble the names of the food groups below and write them on the dashed lines.

_ _ _ _ _ _
F U R I T S

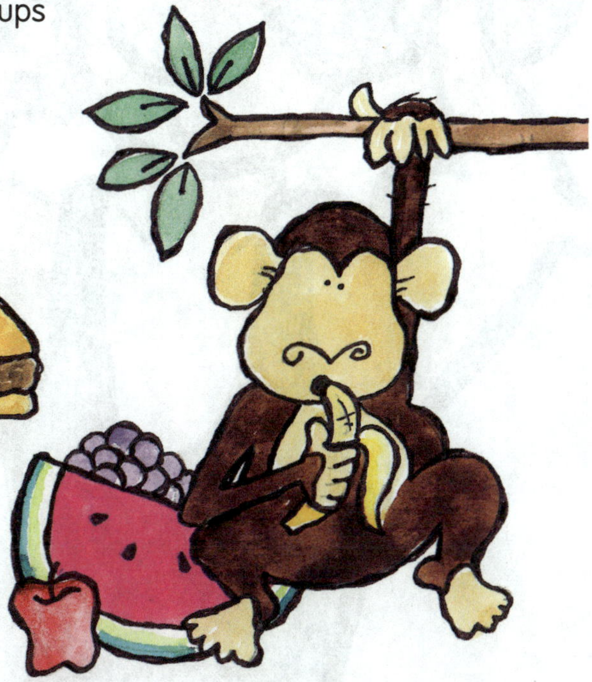

_ _ _ _ _
E M A S T

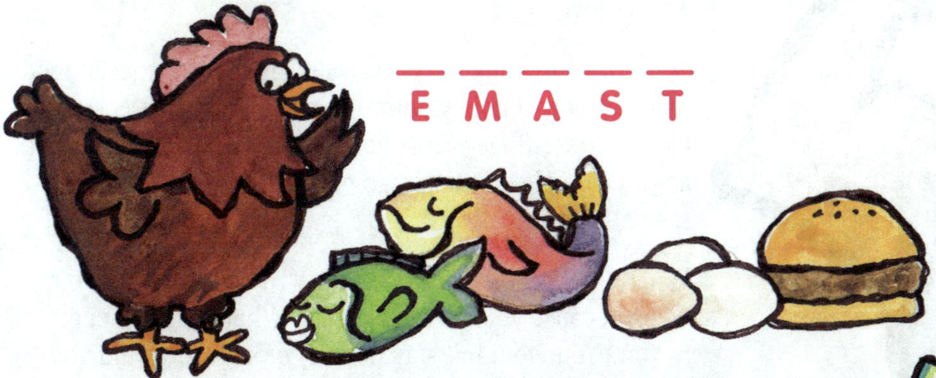

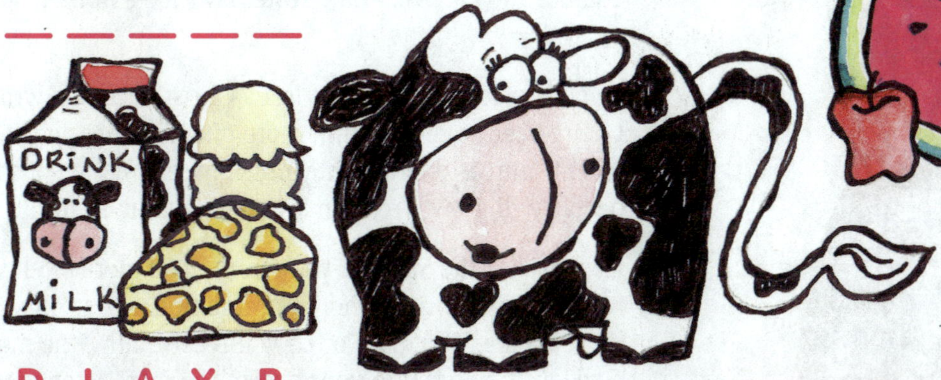

_ _ _ _ _
D I A Y R

DRINK MILK

OATMEAL

_ _ _ _ _ _
G R A I S N

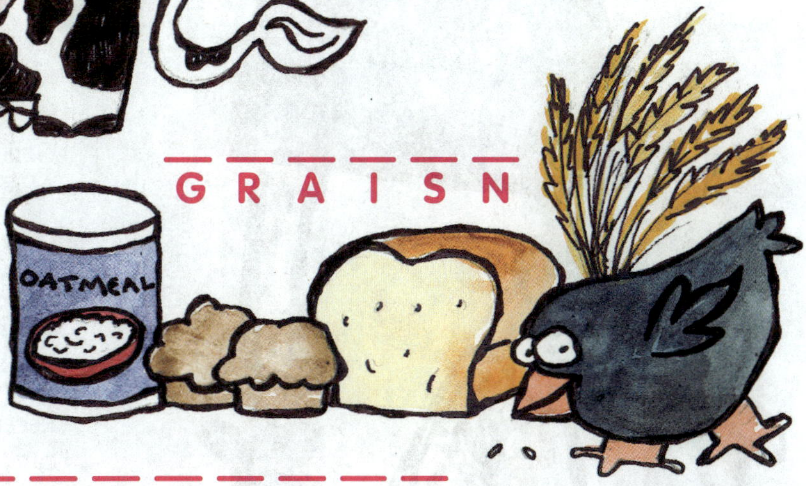

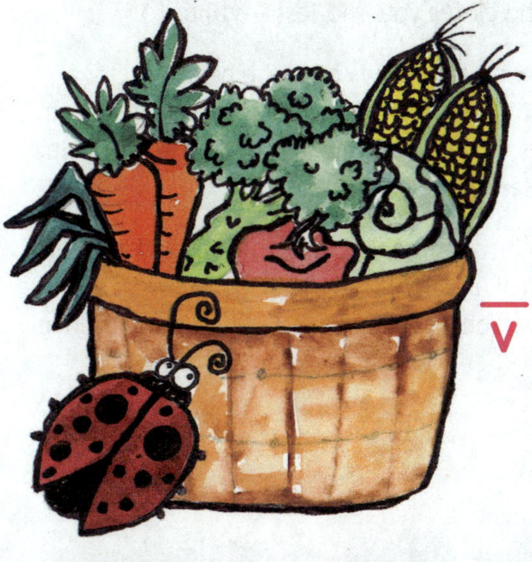

_ _ _ _ _ _ _ _ _ _
V G E T E B A E L S

by Francine M. O'Connor

Lesson 8

Jesus Will Make You Strong

If you had a little puppy, how would you take care of him? Would you feed him every day? Would you give him water to drink? What do you think would happen if you didn't feed your puppy?

Of course, he would get sick. He might even die. Because you love your puppy, you take very good care of him. You give him food and water to keep him strong and healthy.

Your mother and father love you. One way they show their love is by giving you food to eat. They want you to be healthy. They want you to grow up strong.

Jesus loves you very much. He wants you to be strong in a very special way. He wants you to be strong in the Spirit of his love. He wants you to be filled with the love of God the Father. He wants you to love others the way he has always loved you.

To keep you strong in spirit, Jesus gives you a special food. It is the food of holy Communion, the food that is Jesus Christ himself! He wants you to receive this food as often as you can. He wants you to grow strong in this very special way.

What if your mother were to say, "I won't feed you this week because you ate last week?" What would happen to you? You wouldn't stay healthy or strong, would you? You need to eat every day. Yesterday's food won't help you today.

Some people say, "I receive Jesus Christ once in a while. I don't need to receive him more often." Other people receive him as often as they possibly can. Which of these people will grow strong in love and healthy in spirit?

Jesus makes the Spirit in you strong. The more often you receive Jesus Christ in holy Communion, the stronger you will become. The more often you receive him, the more God-love will grow in your heart. The more often you receive him, the closer you and Jesus will be.

Your first holy Communion is only the beginning of a special friendship between you and God. Jesus will help you love others, just the way he loves you. He will help you be kind. He will help you pray.

Receive Jesus Christ in holy Communion whenever you can. Then your wonderful friendship will grow and grow and grow. You and Jesus and God growing in love together.

GROWING WITH JESUS

Jesus gave you the special gift of himself in Communion. Starting at the arrow, read every other letter to see how Jesus wants you to live.

__ __ __ __ __ __ __ __ __ __

__ __ __ __ __ __ __ __ __.

To the Teacher

Perfect examples of people who have walked in God's love can be found in the lives of the saints.

1. Select several saints and read brief synopses of their lives to the children. Some saints who are popular with the children are Saint Therese, Saint Francis, Saint Padre Pio, Saint Bernadette, or the children of Fatima.

2. Ask the children to choose one saint to pattern their lives after this week. Have the children make booklets to record their saint-actions either in words or in pictures.

3. Cut a sheet of plain white paper in half horizontally. Put the two pieces back-to-back, fold in half, and staple in booklet style.

4. The children can decorate the covers of their books with the names and drawings of their chosen saint.

5. Have them list one special attribute of their saint on each of the six inside pages of their books. (For example: Page 1, Francis loved animals. Page 2, Francis was kind to the poor. Page 3, Francis prayed all the time. Page 4, Francis received Jesus Christ in Communion every day. Page 5, Francis taught others to love God. Page 6, Francis loved all living creatures of this world.)

6. Now ask the children to draw pictures or write examples of themselves doing something in imitation of their saint's way of life.

7. The children can use these books to follow the example of their saint all this week.

If approved by the celebrant, collect either the children's saint books or their preparation calendars and make them a part of the Offertory gifts to be presented during their first Communion Mass. These will be each child's personal offering to Jesus on this special day in their lives.

To the Parents

Your child's big day is almost here. First Communion is an exciting and beautiful event. But the excitement and newness can fade quickly unless every encounter with Jesus Christ in Communion is made special. Your own attitude toward the Eucharist is very important to your child's view. Each of you is a saint-in-the-making. A close relationship with Jesus is important to your spiritual progress. Consider the times you receive Jesus Christ in the Eucharist now. Are there opportunities, other than the weekend Mass, for your family to attend Mass? If it is not possible to attend on another regularly scheduled day each week, perhaps you could plan to attend on each family member's birthday or feast day or on some other day that is special to your family. Discuss this possibility in a family meeting.

To help emphasize the growth your child has been making in his or her life, consider making an arrangement of "first" pictures to display at your family celebration of this first Communion day. You can include your child's birth picture, pictures of your child's baptism, first birthday, first steps, first friends, first day of school, and so on.

You can make a collage of the pictures, with a caption below each explaining the event. This is an excellent way to not only recall happy memories but also to show the joy your whole family experiences at one another's special times. Rejoice with your child on this happy day!

From the *Catechism of the Catholic Church*

- #946-48 on the communion of saints
- #1394 on the effects of the Eucharist
- #2013-14 on the Christian call to holiness

Editor: Lauren K. Borstell • Art and design: Christine Kraus

801921

A RIDDLE!

What do you call a group of people who love you
just because you are you, who help you grow up strong and good,
and who teach you about God's love?

Some people have only one of these.

You have two.

Solve the rebus to find the answer to the riddle.

To the Teacher

Make a "We Are One" poster to be displayed in the church on first Communion day. You should discuss this with your Liturgy committee ahead of time. They will help you choose the most convenient place to hang the poster.

You will need:

- Large sheet of poster paper
- Sheet of colored construction paper for each child (use as many different colors as possible)
- Crayons or markers
- Scissors
- Glue
- Ruler
- 12" piece of string

WE ARE ONE

WE RECEIVE JESUS WITH OUR CHURCH FAMILY

Before class, make a light pencil sketch of a loaf of bread on the top half of your poster. Divide this into several puzzle pieces, one for each child in the class. Trace the shapes onto different pieces of colored construction paper to be passed out to the children during class.

1. Above your bread puzzle, print "We Are One" in large letters. In smaller letters, just below your puzzle, write "We receive Jesus with our Church Family."

2. Give each child a colored puzzle piece that you have cut from the construction paper.

3. Ask the children to write their baptismal names on their puzzle pieces.

4. Paste the pieces of the puzzle onto the poster. You now have a multicolored loaf of bread made up of members of the class.

5. You can add lines to the rest of the poster or, in some way, indicate that this space is for the parishioners to add their names.

6. Tape string to the bottom of the poster and tie this securely to a pen or marker.

Your poster is now ready to greet your parish family on first Communion day.

To the Parents

The children are learning that they are an important part of their parish family as well as their home families. Celebrate family this week!

Have a "Memory Night" with your whole family. Using photos, souvenirs, and so forth, help your child relive those family memories that are so important to your unity. Tell your child about the day he or she was baptized — Who was there? What was the name of the priest? What did you do to celebrate? Tell your child how happy you all felt to have brought one more member into God's family.

Plan a family celebration, including as many members of the extended family (grandparents, uncles, aunts, cousins) as possible, for your child's first Communion day. Let your child select how you will celebrate (family picnic, festive meal, cake and ice cream party). Together decide on the menu and (where appropriate) decorations.

If grandparents live too far away to attend your celebration, include them by planning a long-distance call before or after going to the church. This will help emphasize that unity is possible even though miles may separate you.

From the *Catechism of the Catholic Church*

- #790-91 on the Church as one body
- #949 on Church as communion of faith
- #2204-5 on the Christian family

Editor: Lauren K. Borstell • Art and design: Christine Kraus

801921

Picture Crossword

Here are some pictures of things you will see at Mass. Can you find their names in the word list and fill them into the right places in the puzzle?

Word List: paten, host, chalice, candle, altar, pew

To the Teacher

Here is a prayer service to help the children enter more fully into the mystery of the Eucharist.

You will need:

- Elements of Communion — paten, cruets, chalice
- Small card table
- White tablecloth
- Taper to light candles
- Large candle
- Small candle for each, decorated by the children
- Sheet of Styrofoam or clay to hold the small candles
- Bible

Before class, have the table covered and set with the Bible, the taper, and the large candle. Secure the small candles into the Styrofoam or clay and display on the table. Explain the purpose of each Communion item to the children and place it on the table. Have the children gather near the table. Light the large candle.

Have each child come forward and light a small candle from the large one, using the taper. As they are doing this, explain that the Word of God is like a light, brightening the dark corners of their minds. Without the Word of God, they would never have known of the wonderful love that God the Father feels for them.

Have the class sing "God is..." from *ABC's in Song* or a similar song.

Call to Worship

Leader: Father, we have gathered to pray in the name of Jesus your Son. May we be one in our love for you today and every day. And now, as we listen to your Word, help us learn to live and love as your children, through Christ our Lord.

All: Amen

Reading
John 15:9-17

Prayer of Intercession

Leader: Jesus, help us always remember that you died to save us from our sins. For this, we pray to the Lord.

All: Lord, hear our prayer.

Leader: Jesus, help us show others that you live on in our hearts and in our love. For this, we pray to the Lord.

All: Lord, hear our prayer.

Leader: Jesus, we thank you for coming to us in the bread and wine of Communion. Help us stay close to you always. For this, we pray to the Lord.

All: Lord, hear our prayer.

Closing Prayer

Leader: Heavenly Father, you have given us your Son Jesus that we might know your great love. As we prepare to receive our first holy Communion, come fill our hearts with a special desire to embrace our Brother Jesus. We ask this through him, who lives and reigns with you forever.

All: Amen

All sing "I Saw Jesus Today" from *ABC's in Song* or a similar song as the prayer service closes.

To the Parents

This week, help your child make invitations for relatives and friends to join your family on his or her first Communion day. The invitations can be made of plain white sheets of paper. Fold the paper in half from the top, then in half from the side.

Have your child decorate the front of the invitation with his or her own drawings, adding, "Come Celebrate My First Holy Communion."

Since your child will probably be making several invitations, help out by printing a personal invitation on the inside. Include the time of the Mass, location of the church, and so forth.

Discuss with your child how you as a family plan to make this day special. Also, check your child's activities on his or her preparation calendar.

From the *Catechism of the Catholic Church*

- #610-11 on the Last Supper
- #1345-55 on the Liturgy of the Eucharist
- #1391 on Communion and union with Christ

FOR JESUS

GETTING READY FOR JESUS!

You are getting ready to receive Jesus Christ in holy Communion. Before that day comes, you will want to get yourself ready. Unscramble these words and see the two ways Jesus wants you to prepare to receive him. Then fill in the blanks with ways you can follow Jesus' commands.

1. ELVO OGD TWHI LAL UROY AHETR.

____

____

I will show my love for God by saying my ______________________.

I will show my love for God by listening to God's Word at ______________________.

2. ELVO NOE ONAEHTR SA I ELVO OYU.

____

____

I will show my love for others by helping at ______________________.

I will show my love for others by always being ______________________.

To the Teacher

I Prepare for Jesus

As they approach their first holy Communion, it is important that the children prepare themselves to live the Christian life both internally (prayer) and externally (love of neighbor). If you are following this series, there should be just four weeks left until the big day. Preparation should begin now.

Have the children cut out the calendar on the inside of this handout. They will use the calendar to record their preparation activities in either words or pictures. Have the children mark the day of their first Communion with a star or smiling face.

Some suggested preparation activities are listed below. The children can add ideas of their own.

- I am kind to others. • I share my things.
- I am polite. • I help others.
- I clean my room. • I forgive others.
- I say I am sorry. • I show my love.
- I remember my prayers. • I go to Mass.

Each day until the day of their first Communion, the children are to fulfill one of their activities and indicate this on their calendars. Have them take their calendars and hang them where they can add activities as the month progresses.

To the Parents

Today your child will bring home a preparation calendar. Help him or her fulfill the suggested activities each day by providing opportunities for helping, loving, and so forth. These activities will prepare your child in the externals of Chrisitan life, but the establishment of a prayer habit should begin in the home. If you do not have a family prayer time, this could be a good opportunity to start one. Encourage spontaneous prayer during this time.

In addition to spontaneous prayer, you can help your children learn the following traditional prayers by saying them together.

Lord's Prayer

Our Father who art in heaven,
hallowed be thy name.
Thy kingdom come.
Thy will be done on earth,
as it is in heaven.
Give us this day our daily bread,
and forgive us our trespasses,
as we forgive those who trespass against us,
and lead us not into temptation,
but deliver us from evil. Amen

Hail Mary

Hail Mary, full of grace.
The Lord is with you.
Blessed are you among women,
and blessed is the fruit of your womb, Jesus.
Holy Mary, Mother of God,
pray for us sinners,
now and at the hour of our death. Amen

Prayer of Praise

Glory to the Father,
and to the Son,
and to the Holy Spirit;
as it was in the beginning,
is now, and will be forever. Amen

From the *Catechism of the Catholic Church*

• #1698 on life in Christ • #2196 on love of neighbor • #2742-45 on prayer

Editor: Lauren K. Borstell • Art and design: Christine Kraus

JESUS' OWN PRAYER

Once, when Jesus was preaching, someone asked him, "Lord, teach us how to pray." That's when Jesus gave us the Our Father, or the Lord's Prayer. Can you fill in the missing words in Jesus' prayer?

The Lord's Prayer

Our __ __ __ __ __ __ who art in __ __ __ __ __ __,

hallowed be thy __ __ __ __.

Thy __ __ __ __ __ __ __ come.

Thy will be done on __ __ __ __ __ ,

as it is in __ __ __ __ __ __.

Give us this day our daily __ __ __ __ __ ,

and __ __ __ __ __ __ __ us our trespasses as we

forgive those who __ __ __ __ __ __ __ __ against us,

and lead us not into __ __ __ __ __ __ __ __ __ __ ,

but deliver us from __ __ __ __. Amen

Word List:

bread, earth, evil, father, forgive, heaven, heaven, kingdom, name, temptation, trespass

To the Teacher

Understanding the Mass as a family celebration of love of the Father and the self-gift of Jesus is an important part of preparing the children for their first Communion. This week have the children make individual banners that they can take home.

For each child, you will need:

- Drawing paper
- Crayons or markers
- Colored paper
- Scissors
- One 12" piece of yarn or string
- Hole punch

1. Have the children write, "Happy are we who are called to the Lord's Supper" on their banners, leaving room to paste in the chalice and host. Help the children follow the next five steps in the making of their banners.

2. Draw the chalice and host, as above, on colored paper and cut them out. Paste them on the banner.

3. Punch holes in the top right- and left-hand corners.

4. Thread the string or yarn through the holes, knotting it at both ends.

5. Now give the children freedom to walk around the room and have their classmates sign their banners.

Encourage the children to keep their banners as a remembrance of the classmates who shared their preparation to receive Jesus.

To the Parents

In preparation for their first holy Communion, the children are learning the significance of the Mass as a celebration of God's gift and as a reenactment of the Last Supper. Here are some suggestions that might help prepare your child for his or her part in Mass.

- If possible, visit the church sometime during the week. Point out those things your child might miss during Mass — the tabernacle, the vigil candle, the Stations, and so forth. Explain their significance.
- Purchase a picture missal at your local Catholic bookstore. Read the book with your child and identify the different sections of the Mass.
- Before Mass, read and discuss the gospel and the readings with your child. Help him or her identify with the message.
- Arrive at Mass early! Sit as close to the sanctuary as possible. Nothing turns a child off faster than to see nothing but the backs of people's heads.
- Set an example of the spiritual attitude necessary for Mass by your own prayerful attention. Join heartily in the prayer responses and singing. Encourage your child to do the same.
- Encourage your child to follow the Mass in the picture missal or, if your child's reading ability is advanced enough and if your parish provides them, a missalette.
- On the way home from Mass, discuss the gospel message. Think of ways you can fit this into your lives.

From the *Catechism of the Catholic Church*

- #1341, 1356-57 on Communion as a memorial celebration
- #1342-44 on Mass as center of Church's life
- #2770 on the Lord's Prayer

Editor: Lauren K. Borstell

Art and design: Christine Kraus

801921

A PROMISE FROM JESUS

Jesus makes you a wonderful promise.
Using the key below, can you decode his message?

__ __   __ __ __   __ __ __   __ __ __   __ __ __ __ __
A B   E F D   G C H   H J A I   K L G C M

__ __ __   __ __ __ __ __   __ __ __ __
E F D   I J C N N   N A O G

__ __ __ __ __ __ __.
P F L G O G L

Key:

A=I; B=F; C=A; D=U; E=Y; F=O; G=E; H=T; I=S; J=H; K=B; L=R; M=D; N=L; O=V; P=F

To the Teacher

The consolation and promise of Jesus at the Last Supper (John 14) is one of the most beautiful passages in the Bible. We have taken selections from this passage and broken them into ten readings. Have the children take turns reading the different parts. If there are more than ten children in the class, the passages can be further broken down.

Child One: "Don't be worried! Have faith in God and have faith in me. There are many rooms in my Father's house. I wouldn't tell you this, unless it was true. I am going there to prepare a place for each of you. After I have done this, I will come back and take you with me. Then we will be together. You know the way to where I am going" (1-4).

Child Two: "Lord, we don't even know where you are going! How can we know the way?" (5).

Child Three: "I am the way, the truth, and the life! Without me, no one can go to the Father. If you had known me, you would have known the Father" (6-7).

Child Four: "Lord, show us the Father. That is all we need" (8).

Child Five: "Philip, I have been with you for a long time. Don't you know who I am? If you have seen me, you have seen the Father" (9).

Child Six: "The Father who lives in me does these things. Ask me, and I will do whatever you ask" (10,13).

Child Seven: "If you love me, you will do what I have said, and my Father will love you. I will also love you and show you what I am like" (21).

Child Eight: "If anyone loves me, they will obey me. Then my Father will love them, and we will come to them and live in them" (23).

Child Nine: "The Spirit will teach you everything and will remind you of what I said while I was with you" (26).

Child Ten: "I give you peace, the kind of peace that only I can give. It isn't like the peace that this world can give. So don't be worried or afraid" (27).

After the reading, discuss these passages with the children. Ask them how Jesus' words and promises make them feel, which passage talks about heaven, the Holy Spirit, and so forth. Help them recognize that these promises were made to all of us.

To the Parents

To emphasize this week's lesson with your child, take time to read a biblical account of the Last Supper (Mt 26:26-30 or Mk 14:22-26). Discuss how Jesus shares himself with us in this special way so that he can live and work through us, just as God the Father lived and worked through Jesus.

Ask your child to list several ways that he or she can share himself or herself with others (making friends, sharing toys, helping at home).

Now ask your child to add to the list some ways that he or she can share himself or herself with God (praying, going to Mass, keeping the commandments).

Ask your child to keep the list where he or she can look at it every day, to help him or her grow in love for God and for neighbor.

Help your child learn and say the following prayer during Communion at Mass.

Communion Prayer

Jesus Christ in the Communion bread,
I know that you are really here.
I've come especially because
I always love to have you near.

When I receive you in my heart,
I feel your Presence ever dear.
Jesus Christ in the Communion bread,
bless your child who's kneeling here.

From the *Catechism of the Catholic Church*

- #151 on belief in Jesus
- #610-11 on the Last Supper
- #661 on Jesus as access to heaven
- #2615 on Jesus' teachings on prayer

Editor: Lauren K. Borstell

Art and design: Christine Kraus

801921

t from Jesus

HE BREAD OF LIFE.

Jesus fed thousands of people with a few loaves of bread. The people were surprised and happy. They had been hungry but now they were full. "This bread is a gift of God," they thought, "a gift of love for the people."

Jesus fed the people with bread. But he had more to tell them. *"I am the Bread of Life,"* he said. "No one who comes to me will ever be hungry. No one who has faith in me will ever be thirsty" (Jn 6:35). The people did not understand. "How can a man be bread?" they wondered.

"I am the Bread of Life." It is a strange saying. It is a mysterious saying. It is a saying filled with love.

When the people were hungry, Jesus gave them bread to eat. But people need more than bread. People need God's love. People need God's life. People need a gift that lasts forever. Jesus was talking about the gift of himself, the true "Bread of Life."

How can Jesus be bread? If you are hungry for food, bread will fill your hunger. But you have other kinds of hunger. When you are sad and hungry for love, Jesus can fill your heart with his love. When you are lonesome, hungry for friends, you have Jesus to talk to in your prayers. When you make a mistake, when you are angry, or when you get mixed up about right or wrong, Jesus will forgive you. He will teach you how to be good.

"I am the Bread of Life." Jesus is the Bread of Life. He will fill all your hungers. He will help you to be good. He will be with you every day of your life. This is the wonderful gift that you will receive soon: Jesus Christ himself, in the Communion Bread. Remember what Jesus said, "Everyone who eats [the Bread of Life] will live forever. My flesh is the life-giving bread that I give to the people of this world" (Jn 6:51).

To the Teacher

The gift that Jesus gives in holy Communion is the gift of himself. A parent may give the gift of himself or herself by fixing a special meal for the family, or by helping the children with their homework. A teacher may give the gift of himself or herself by encouraging children to learn. This week, help the children find new ways to give the gift of themselves to others by making personal coupon books explaining their gifts.

The children will need:

- 3" x 5" index cards, at least six per child
- Hole punch
- Markers
- 6" to 8" pieces of yarn

THIS COUPON ENTITLES YOU TO…

____

____

TO:____________ **FROM:**____________

Direct the children in the following steps:

1. On one index card, have each child write: "I give the gift of myself." The children can make this the cover and decorate it with pictures and designs.

2. Punch a small hole at the top, left-hand corner of the cards and tie them together with the yarn, keeping the decorated card on top.

3. Discuss together the many ways that the children can give of themselves. Some ideas are: help Mom with the dishes; make a card for a person who is sick or lonely; share a toy with a friend. Encourage the children to come up with ideas for themselves.

4. On the top of each of the remaining index cards have the children print: "This coupon entitles you to..."

5. Now have the children write a gift of self on each coupon. If they have trouble coming up with enough gifts to fill all their coupons, remind them that some gifts can be given more than once.

6. Be sure the children leave one line at the bottom of their coupon to fill in the name of the person they will give the coupon to — Mom, Dad, Grandma, Susie, Tommy.

7. Tell the children that each time they give a coupon and complete their gift of self, they can write that gift on a leaf and paste it on their Jesus Tree.

To the Parents

Most children are accustomed to thinking of a gift as something material. Before your child can fully appreciate holy Communion as Jesus' "gift of himself," you need to help him or her understand how a person can be a gift.

The things you do every day, things your child may take for granted, are truly gifts of self. You can identify these gifts by saying, "Today my gift to you is..." and tell your child what you have done "just because I love you."

Other events can also be examined and identified as gifts of self. If a neighbor does something special for you or any member of the family, explain how that neighbor has given a gift of self. Talk about the missionaries whose whole lives are gifts of self to God. Tell your child of Mother Teresa, whose gift of self was given daily to the suffering people of India.

Read John 14:18-21, in which Jesus promises to live on in each of us. Explain that Jesus keeps that promise by giving the gift of himself through holy Communion.

From the *Catechism of the Catholic Church*

- #519-21 on the mysteries of Jesus
- #655 on the significance of Jesus' Resurrection
- #1333-35 on the signs of bread and wine
- #1351 on the collection of gifts

Editor: Lauren K. Borstell

Art and design: Christine Kraus

801921

START
SMILE CORNER
JESUS KIND OF LOVE
MUST FLIP TAILS TO WIN
HUG CORNER
HIGH-FIVE CORNER

To the Teacher

Make a Jesus Tree

This Jesus Tree can be used throughout preparation for first Communion. For the tree, each child will need:

- Large piece of poster board
- Crayons or markers
- Green, orange, and yellow construction paper
- Large envelope
- Glue

Direct the children through the following steps:

1. On the poster board, draw a large tree without leaves. Color the tree brown.

2. Beneath the tree, write, "We love as Jesus loves."

3. Cut green, orange, and yellow leaves out of construction paper. You will need enough leaves to fill the branches of the tree.

4. On one side of the green leaves, write, "Forgiving." On the yellow leaves, write, "Healing." On the orange leaves, write, "Feeding."

5. Each child should have an envelope filled with several leaves of each color.

6. After you have discussed the lesson, explain to the children that it will be up to them to fill the tree with leaves. Every time a child loves in a Jesus way, he or she can sign the back of a colored leaf that corresponds to the action and glue it on the tree.

As the weeks go by, the children can watch their Jesus Tree blossom because of their love and kindness. Some of their love deeds can be class projects (adding to a collection box for the poor or writing cards for the sick in hospitals and for seniors in retirement homes). Others can be done at home or on their own (forgiving each other, sharing with their friends, or helping around the house).

To the Parents

As the children prepare to receive Jesus in their first holy Communion, they will be striving to live more and more as Jesus lived. You are in the best position to help and guide your child in his or her spiritual growth. Each night this week, read one of the following seven Bible passages to your child. The passages are short so you can allow time to discuss Jesus' action and how your child can adapt that action to his or her life. The more your child learns about Jesus and his way of love, the more meaningful the celebration of this sacrament will be.

Passages of love: Mt 8:5-13; 9:1-8; 9:18-25; 9:27-31; Mk 8:31-37; 10:46-52; Lk 9:10-17.

From the *Catechism of the Catholic Church*

- #544 on Jesus preaching to the "poor"
- #545 on Jesus' invitation to sinners
- #588-89 on Jesus' mercy toward and forgiveness of sinners
- #1503-05 on Christ the physician

Editor: Lauren K. Borstell

Art and design: Christine Kraus

ISBN 978-0-7648-0192-1